# Mental Health Recovery Book

**An expose by the mother of a son with schizophrenia including care, nutrition and living within the family unit**

*by Kaye Dennan*

ISBN: 978-1492171324

# Table of Contents

# 1. Dedication

Dedicated to my loving family, my son's father

and all the Mental Health Workers, Doctors and

Carers

who have been a tremendous support

throughout this amazing journey.

# 2. Introduction

As of writing this book....

This book has been written by Kaye Dennan, a mother of a son who has been diagnosed with paranoid/schizophrenia.

For 10 years the family has been through all sorts of ups and downs trying to come to terms with this illness and how to best manage the situation for all concerned. There have been many trials and errors, laughter and tears, hopes soaring and hopes dashed, but we have embraced this journey and I believe have become stronger for the experience.

At the end you will read how things are 5 years on....

From the very first I would like to welcome you into my world and the world of thousands of families around the globe who have a family member with a psychiatric disorder.

The journey has not been all bad. Oh, yes, there certainly have been times that I would rather not have experienced but, hey, this is it and I love my son unconditionally.

The purpose behind this book is to open the eyes of carers who may or may not face some of the situations that either I have experienced or that some of my fellow carers have suffered.

Sadly, this ebook may be a shock to read for those who are 'new carers', as the facts were to me when I realized we were dealing with a probable lifelong mental illness, not just juvenile bad behavior. Let me tell you, this realization did not hit for about 2 years after we knew we had a problem on our hands and then I had to go through the long and arduous task of learning how to cope.

You know, I am 'just a mum', trying to do the best for my son who has been inflicted with paranoid/schizophrenia. It has been 10 years now that the family has been dealing with this illness and it certainly has felt like a roller coaster ride. The highs and lows, the expectations, the disappointments, the frustration and of course, all the arguments and tears certainly had an impact. At times I felt these experiences would never end.

**BUT I AM HAPPY TO SAY MY SON AND THE FAMILY HAVE COME TO A REASONABLY HAPPY PLACE IN LIFE RIGHT NOW.**

It must be pointed out that I have *never officially studied mental illness or have ever taken any medical studies.* I have just listened to carers, doctors, health care workers and anybody who I felt knew a bit about mental illness. **I did take on the**

**role of a facilitator at a carers group for 3 years** where I learnt about coping, helping, counseling and so much more.

Any thoughts you may develop from this book I would encourage you to confirm with your doctors and counselors because each case is individual in its own unique way.

I am not here to judge either myself or anyone who is in the carer's role, as I know that all you can do is make decisions in the moment, sometimes knowing they are right and sometimes **just hoping** they are right, only to be proven wrong at a later date. Experience plays a huge role in this learning curve.

After 10 years of family struggles and my son learning to cope with this illness he is now living in a self contained 'granny flat' on the ground floor of our house and coping quite well with most aspects of his life. I don't know if he will ever work again as his memory and concentration is poor, but I would have to say his life is not too bad when I think about what it was like for him during the previous 10 years.

*For the sake of this book when I refer to 'carer' I am referring to someone as a carer for a person with a psychiatric illness as opposed to someone with an intellectual mental disability or a physical disability. The carers role in those situations is quite different again and I have no experience there.*

My thoughts have probably been colored by my experience with schizophrenia but I hope you will find the general information very helpful in dealing with your own situation if dealing with a mentally ill family member.

Everybody's journey is different, some better than others, some easy to cope with and some just devastating and my love and compassion goes to those who are finding it so hard to cope.

All I can say is that if you feel that you have a family member that is doing **'odd'** things, things that you don't feel are normal, or has **'odd'** behavior , then start taking steps and seek help.  The sooner these issues can be addressed the better because the longer without treatment the harder it is to get well. The reality is though, that initially we live in a world of 'wonder':

- wonder if something is wrong
- wonder if it will change
- wonder if he/she will get better
- wonder if it's just an age thing, as in teenage behavior
- wonder if there has been something that has triggered some odd behavior

Some of these illnesses can make someone ill for a short period of time then all seems well again until next time there is an episode. That is why it is so hard to make a final commitment to facing the problem.

We all want to believe there is nothing wrong, and if we have not been exposed to mental health issues before, may not even realize that these behaviors are signs of a mental illness.

# 3. Diagnosis

It can often be years before a mental illness is diagnosed because so many symptoms can present the same and sometimes a person can suffer from several symptoms of several illnesses.

Also, there are other issues, such as the person who is ill may not at the time of assessment, be able to communicate the problems they face and therefore the diagnosis could be wrong. That is why there are usually several assessments before doctors are prepared to label an illness and this can take several months or even years.

It is so important though that you get an accurate diagnosis as soon as possible so that everyone can start working on the process of getting life back on track.

Once you have the diagnosis, try and get all the facts about the illness you are dealing with as soon as possible because, I believe, the more you understand what the sufferer is going through the more you will be able to understand and set up a situation to cope.

It can be very frustrating when you can't get a diagnosis because you don't know what you are dealing with.  At first I just thought a lot of what was going on with my son was plain bad behavior or at the other extreme an introverted personality as he started keeping to himself a lot and staying in his room for hours on end.

Two years and two hospitalizations had gone by before we were given a diagnosis.  Once I was told I felt I just had to deal with it and learn more about it.  On the one hand, the diagnosis was a bit horrifying in itself, but on the other hand, it explained a lot of what had been happening and that was a relief.

Fortunately, these days there is a lot of information on the internet, but I would caution that a psychiatric illness is not a 'black and white' illness, so don't expect it to present exactly as you read about.   The internet is beneficial for getting more information about an illness, rather than trying to diagnose an illness.

**I must stress that often when someone is very unwell they DO NOT EVEN KNOW THEY ARE UNWELL.**

**When we, as carers, are dealing with them we are dealing from a rational point of view and they are dealing from their own reality which would most likely be nothing like ours.**

## 4. Be prepared for all eventualities

First and foremost, once you know you are definitely dealing with a mental illness disorder get all the knowledge you can about the particular illness. Find out all the contact phone numbers and addresses of the services in your area. That is, the services for the mentally ill person and also the services available for the carer.

It is so important that both needs are catered for, if not now maybe later, but get this information as soon as possible and keep it all together somewhere.

Make sure that you have emergency numbers if you are dealing with someone who can be at risk to themselves or others because you never know when you may need it.

Find **yourself** a counselor that you can talk to and a counselor that your **loved one** can relate to. This may or may not be the same person. Do use their services if the home front gets too touchy and you need help negotiating some home rules.

You can often end up in a very volatile situation and need extra help to calm things down. It is amazing how a third party can help calm things down and keep situations under control.

Seek out a good psychiatrist, especially one that your loved one relates to. In saying that, it is quite common that a person with a mental illness does not see the psychiatrist as a helpful person and often doesn't want to talk to them.

You may have to find a few over the years if necessary. The psychiatrists are the ones imposing restrictions, sending them to hospital and basically seen as the person who is trying to 'read their brain'.

Depending on your country's mental health services you may get government paid assistance or you may have to go private.

When you do find a counselor and a psychiatrist, don't be shy, just ask them straight out what they are going to do for you! How are they going to help you!

Before you go to meetings with any health care people make sure that you are prepared with your questions beforehand. The life of a carer can be very disorganized at times due to unforeseen events, so you need to learn to plan ahead.

The meetings can often jump from one topic to another as the patient's thoughts scramble around so it is helpful to take your questions so that you can ensure they get answered. Sometimes even phone or email them ahead.

Find out if there are any mental health educational programs going on in your area for either yourself or your loved one as these will be invaluable to help you understand and find solutions.

Rehabilitation can be a long process so the more information you have at hand the better.  I have heard it said that:

 *When a person with a mental illness reaches 30+ they seem to take on the attitude that life is passing them by with nothing to show for it and that they had better start working on themselves*.

I must say that I have actually seen this happen to a number of people and believe there may well be some truth in it.

I would suggest that if a person over 18 suffers from a mental illness then it would pay to familiarize yourself with a Power of Attorney form which can be downloaded off the internet just in case you feel it will be needed down the track. The law varies in different countries so you would need to familiarize yourself with what exactly you would need and the restrictions which may be placed on you.

There are actually two forms: Enduring Power of Attorney and the Power of Attorney. Check out which one would suit your circumstances.

**Believe in yourself**, you will make mistakes as we all do, but you will also do some very good things.

**Don't let anyone tell you different**.

# 5. Medication

As I said in the Introduction I do not have any association with the medical profession so I will not elaborate too much here except to say that my belief is that medication is extremely important when trying to get someone well again after being affected with a mental illness.

As to the long term use of medications that would obviously need to be addressed by the doctors involved. Not everyone agrees to taking medication and for some that may be the answer.

Most, if not all, medications have side effects of some sort and it is important that you know what these are and possible ways to counteract them if possible.

If a person is suffering a severe mental disorder and needs to be taking other medication for other illnesses, such as diabetes, it is important that these are monitored because when someone is in a mentally unstable condition it is likely that medications will be overlooked which then exacerbates the whole general well being.

The aim of anti-psychotic medications is to slow the brain down so that a person can reasonably cope with the illness and also relax them so that they can sleep.

# 6. Stigma of mental illness

I must say that this was never one of my major
problems.  But in saying that, we are not madly
social people and the way I saw it was if I told
someone that we were dealing with a mental
illness, and they didn't like it, too bad for them.

Just because I felt that way it doesn't of course
mean to say my son felt the same way.

When out and about and feeling that people are
looking at them because of their odd behavior,
speech or dress, those who have a mental illness
do often become fearful and if they suffer from
paranoia this can become a real problem.

**In trying to get my son to accept the illness, I
used to liken it to a heart attack or liver disease**.
In other words, an organ of the body that is not

functioning properly and therefore needs medication to get the function back on track.

I used these examples because our family has a history of heart attacks, but use whatever will have type of illness that needs to be managed..

I try not to 'walk on eggshells' regarding the illness and I know in life in general I might flippantly say things like 'she was so crazy' or such like, but so many terms like this are used at times and they don't really mean anything specific.

You will find yourself saying things that you would have said before without even thinking about it relating to anyone. To me that is just one of the ways we have to be ourselves and move on.

Don't get too hung up on this stuff, there are other many more important issues to deal with.

# 7. Communication

Trying to communicate with a sufferer can be **very** difficult at times. I often find, even now, that when I am talking to my son he is not listening. He has learnt to appear as if he is, but when I stop talking he hasn't even realized I have done so.

With all the activity going on in their head [which could be **racing thoughts, voice activity or paranoia distraction**] they may not hear what you are saying and, of course, won't take in, or remember what you are saying.

Until I understood this, I used to find it **TOTALLY FRUSTRATING**, in fact, one of the hardest things to cope with on an ongoing daily basis. I felt I was always repeating myself.

**With this knowledge, I have learnt so much more patience** and **it has changed our relationship** around dramatically. I used to lose my cool because I always had to keep repeating myself, but now that I understand why it happens, I bite my lip, repeat myself, and **check for acknowledgement**.

By acknowledgement I mean checking with them to see if they understand what it is you were wanting. If you ask "did you hear me?" they say "yes", but in reality they possibly didn't and then you are back at square one getting agitated again. It's better to **ask them to repeat the task you desire done** or query what you told them, which will probably get a grumble from them, but at least you will know where you are with the issue.

Even with someone who is very ill at the time there are still windows of opportunity where you can hold a quick conversation and discuss issues that need addressing. This is very important when they are suffering quite a long period of illness because there are matters that you do need to get acknowledgement about from them.

Remember they are intellectually affected, and can possibly still make rational decisions when they are reasonably well.

**Pick your times and pick your most important topics to discuss.**

It is often a good idea to write down what it is that you want and leave them a note so that when the time is right action can be taken, i.e. but make sure you put the note somewhere where it will not get lost or covered up, like on a table. It is a good idea to have a cork board for communication notes.

# 8. The illness and the person

Many years after we had been trying to cope I remember one health care worker saying, "There is **bad behavior** and there is the **illness**. They are two entirely different things."

With this information we started to take a different view as to what was happening around the house. At times I found it so difficult to distinguish between the two.

As carers we all witness different behaviors and in each family we all have different acceptances of general behavior, but I do believe there is a difference between the bad behavior and the illness that should be addressed to make living conditions at home more acceptable. After all they are living with you, not you with them.

My instinct was certainly to keep the family peace and to do this I often gave into my son but on looking back that really only extended the time of the bad behavior. It would have been better if I faced the issue sooner rather than later. I had to train myself to take a hard line as I am a very empathetic person and found it hard to be hard! Eventually though, I had to for the sake of my own health.

Also when faced with many of these issues in the early days you hope they will go away, but in reality they don't and all the hope in the world does not change the circumstances, it is only by taking action that anything can change.

# 9. How do carers cope?

## To be the best carer you need to learn how to care for yourself

### The Early Stages

I will always remember the very first time my son was hospitalized, it is imprinted on my mind forever.

It was when we had taken my son to the general hospital because he was doing strange things that my first horror was experienced.

My son had gone into the emergency ward and was being seen by the doctors who asked us to wait outside. As we (I was with my daughter) waited I saw this wire cage attached to the hospital building and wondered what it was for, animals or what? "That's strange," I thought.

After his consultation I was told he was going to be admitted to the psychiatric unit and then when I visited him "the cage" was the outside area where the patients could go and smoke. You can imagine my horror at such a traumatic time.

As time has gone by I have come to realize that if the hospital system is good in your area then when they are really unwell this can usually be the best place for them. It is safe, it is structured, it is monitored and they don't feel fearful or feel threatened as they can on the outside. Sure, they may be on stronger medicated levels than usual but this is because they have been very unwell and the medication levels in the body need to be brought back up so that they can function properly again.

Also once they have become this unwell they have possibly not slept well for a long time and so the rest is badly needed.

In fact I have heard of cases where there is no family involvement and the patients purposely do things so that they get picked up by the police to get put back into hospital and feel safe again.

The early stages of the illness can be horrifying as the family comes to terms with what is being dealt with. It often takes longer for the person suffering from the illness to come to terms with the fact they have a serious mental illness and this can lead to a lot of the problems that you hear of and read about.

It can take years adjusting medication, being consistent with medication and learning to live within their abilities.

## Guilt

Although I know a lot of people, especially mothers, who feel guilty that their son/daughter has a mental illness. *PLEASE*, try not to waste your valuable energy on this emotion. I know it can be crippling going down this path but unless someone has actually become ill in a situation where it can be related to a certain life experience (eg. Death in the family, financial crisis, car accident etc) it is very difficult to know how it all began, and once it has, the best thing you can do is learn and guide them through to recovery.

## Anger and Frustration

Usually everybody in the family shows anger and frustration at some time or another. It is a fact that with a psychiatric patient the anger can present in various forms from quite drastic and life threatening, to a bit of yelling and door slamming, or even quite the opposite just walking away and no-one knowing where they have gone.

Not meaning to be discriminatory here, but men (the male family carer) seem to do more of the physical violence stuff (not necessarily against another person) which is a normal typical male thing anyway, with women showing their anger in other ways.

The demonstration of anger by anyone in the family (if it is related to the illness) is a way of an outlet as they try to come to terms with the illness. This anger may only last a while or it may go on for a long time depending on many factors.

Paranoia, voice and constant activity in the brain can cause huge problems for a person with a mental illness. This makes it very difficult for the carer to understand.

It is helpful to acknowledge this anger between parties because often it is not even recognized as a sign of coming to terms with the illness, and this can purely and simply be because everyone is so caught up in trying to cope that they haven't had time to realize why they are so angry.

## Stress and Tension

These are feelings that become second nature in the early stages of the illness. Because the illnesses can have the sufferers changing in attitude from one minute, one second to the next, tension can run rife. Over time you most likely will be able to control some of these outbursts by early intervention of the situation or even just understanding why the situation arose and then dealing with it appropriately, or at least the best way you can.

The very best way for a person with a mental illness to achieve any rehabilitation is to be living in a reasonably stress free environment.  This can be very difficult to achieve if the whole family is not operating with the same thoughts and goals in mind.

Someone with a mental illness doesn't need to be treated as if they are fragile like someone getting over a heart attack, but certainly there will need to be some changes  in the household to accommodate the needs of an ill family member: eg. quiet space, peaceful time to relax (which is so important to someone who is dealing with an illness), leaving them alone if they go to their room for seclusion.

**Carers Need Time Out**

It is so important that carers take some time out for themself to relax.  It may only be ½ hour a day, but take it and take it for yourself unreservedly!

Whether it be a long hot shower, a bit of gardening, a walk around the block or a favorite TV program, take it and enjoy it AND DON'T LET YOURSELF BE INTERRUPTED.  It is very hard to find this time and may take some planning, some selfishness, or just plain ignoring everyone else around you, *but try and find the time*.

I found the morning quite good because often those with an illness stay up late at night and sleep well into the morning if they are unwell, so this can be a good time JUST FOR YOU!

If you are at a stage of caring for someone when things just seem so hopeless, keep in mind the fact that it will change, no two days will be the same.

Live one day at a time. Deal with the HERE AND NOW and don't waste too much energy on the future, the future can look after itself.  Sometimes if you look at too big a picture it can all seem too overwhelming.

**Strategies For Your Own Self Care**

As the carer it pays to keep in mind that if you go down healthwise, then there will be no-one to look after you and there will be no-one to look after your loved one, so it is very important that *you look after yourself at the outset*.

- don't get lost in the whole illness routine, i.e. try to keep your daily routine and theirs separate and don't let them 'dangle you on a string like a puppet' because they will try
- when negativity is all around you, often created by others, try not to feel responsible for their behavior as you will most likely get accused of things that you did (and may

have even done) but you have done it to be helpful, but it has not been taken in that light

- try and get regular exercise to get some of those 'feel good' endorphins running around your body > you might need to get

- a 'buddy' to help keep you motivated, it could be a family member or even another carer

- involve yourself in a rewarding hobby or some sort of other interest, hard to do yes, but find something that may only take 15-20 mins such as coloring or such like

- try and maintain some sort of social life, even if you feel you don't want to bring people home, you can always meet elsewhere

- look to carers groups or mental health educational groups for support and suggestions on coping

- try to walk away from heated arguments and re-approach those problems when emotions are not running high

- learn to count to 10 (such an old theory) if tempers are frazzled > someone who is suffering from delusions could be angry one minute and quite OK the next when the delusions have subsided > look for signs of distress in them and realize that it is probably not really you they are angry at

- name calling can be a problem, especially someone who suffers from delusions (it could even be the voices telling them what to say) so try and establish this and don't allow bad behavior to develop under the guise of an illness – if you feel they are name calling and not delusional make it known that you won't accept that behavior (it is probably their outlet for their frustrations)
- don't give empty threats, think consequences through and if you are going to threaten to enforce behavior make sure you are prepared to follow through > this will mean that you stay in control which is so important > don't give away your authority
- keep reassessing your situation and make sure you are not 'living' the illness > by this I

mean don't let their illness affect your life as much as it is theirs > **sounds selfish? no it's not**, if you let the illness affect your life as much as theirs what use are you going to be to them in helping them get well


**Trying to See The Funny Side**

If anyone had told me in the early stages that I would be laughing about some of the things that had happened I wouldn't have believed them. I found the carer's meetings great for coping strategies, but also as a means of stress relief where you could openly talk to people who understood what you are going through, and even have a chuckle at some of the ridiculous things that have happened.

The other day my son and I were out having a coffee and we had a chuckle over a couple of the incidents that had occurred over the past years.

Even he said, "Gee, I was off my head then, wasn't I?" It's lovely to hear him recognize those moments because it means he is well enough to look back on those times and reflect where he is now.

I tell you, **there is one skill you will need to learn real fast** and that is to **become the best negotiator around.**

Life becomes 'a little bit your way, a little bit my way'. Most of the carers I know found this a way of coping rather than trying to get it all their way. After a while a lot of carers even turn this negotiating thing into a bit of a game – it certainly does add a bit of fun to it AND **a lot of personal satisfaction if you win one!**

## Expectations

**This was a great lesson for me and a big turning point in my coping!**

Of course you have expectations, don't we all?   For years I used to believe that my son was going to do this, going to do that and the story went on and on and on and still does. I was living in hope that everything was going to change.

**I convinced myself to believe anything.**

But, alas **I was disappointed time after time**, and each time the hurt just seemed to get harder to take and the hopelessness set in deeper and deeper. **The next learning curve** for me came at a time when I was just about to give up.

Someone once said to me **"don't have any expectations and you won't be disappointed"**. I thought, "how could I not, this is the only way I can exist, believing he was going to get better NOW". Soon after being told this I started putting the **"don't have expectations"** thing into practice. At first it was a bit hard, but in only few weeks **it had an immense effect on my stress levels.**

**I was back in control – I could choose to believe it or not**. I learnt that if I didn't expect it, I didn't get disappointed and then I did not reflect this in anger and frustration at my son.

*Don't expect, but celebrate and praise when it does happen!*

It really was such a simple thing and it had an amazing effect on me and my stress levels. **This was one of the milestones for me.**

# 10. Understanding voices by experimentation

What do I mean by voices?  Hallucinations and delusions are part of the psychotic illness and 'voices' are the most common form of hallucination. Voices can be a frightening experience as they are often unpleasant and may cause the person to lose touch with reality or distort their view of the world around them.

Not everyone who is psychiatrically ill suffers from hearing voices, but they are often the cause of the paranoia that creates so much trouble.

When someone is hearing voices it is exactly as if someone nearby is speaking to them.  The experience for them **is amazingly life-like** and usually the person hearing the voices is totally convinced that anyone in the room can also hear the same thing!   The reaction of the person hearing the voices depends on what is being 'said'.  The voices can be loving, revolting, instructional, self deprecating, sexual, racial, humorous or any other normal vocal experience.

The voices may continue 24/7 and if they do, the sufferer really has a very, very hard time dealing with it and by the end of the day they are completely exhausted.  It is a reaction to the voices that often causes a lot of the yelling and screaming that you may hear from someone who is suffering.

Can you imagine being forced to listen to say, music that you don't like all day long, without a break and no way of turning it off!

Recently I did a Recovery Course about the experience of living with voices from the perspective of someone with a lived experience.  I would truly recommend this as a family exercise if your loved one suffers from voices.   It was an eye opening exercise.

The idea of the exercise is to experience hearing voices for a long period of time whilst you are trying to do other every day chores.  For some it is quite difficult and most people found it very tiring to

have constant voices going on.  It certainly gives you a very different idea of what someone is going through if they have to live with that 24/7.  You can see why they are so tired and everything is just overwhelming.

 I found I was actually starting to make the same humming noises as on the tape which showed me what it is like when we see people making all sorts of noises and talking to themselves.

If you wanted to try this exercise you would need to have some voices recorded that vary from whispering to strong language, musical voices through to snappy voices, pleasant sayings to nasty and crude sayings.

The exercise involves a person having the headphones on for about 2 hours and during that time do an assortment of tasks, ranging from shopping, filling out forms, reading and other everyday activities.

The idea is to be in pairs so if the person with the earphones leaves the house the buddy can see to their safety and oversee what they do without any interference. But even if you did this around the house for a couple of hours you would see how difficult it is to hold a conversation, watch TV or do other chores like filling out forms or writing letters when the voice from the headphones is constant.

**Motivation and the activity of constant voices** can be a major reason why someone who is mentally ill sits around all day and appears to be lazy.

I know we thought my son was lazy and so did the extended family. If you keep saying to someone who is ill that they are lazy it can be quite upsetting if the sitting around is caused by the head activity.

A mental illness will most likely demotivate a person anyway and psychotic medication demotivates them even more. That is one reason why people who are on quite a high dose of medication appear to be lethargic and uninterested in things.

# 11. It's all about me

Both carer and sufferer start to live in a world of self-importance. I believe that this comes about by each trying to cope with what has been dished out to them.

Neither want to be in the situation they are in, and neither of them can cope.

The carer may start to suffer from all sorts of stress related illnesses so their life becomes very important to them as they try to cope and the sufferer can only think of themselves as their health deteriorates and as they try and cope. There is no way the sufferer can even start thinking about anybody else as they can't even help themselves! To stay focused and get through the day is more than they can often deal with.

This is often when a marriage will be under tremendous stress, or even other siblings feel their parents are pulling away and have no time for them.

AND, I believe that both have a very valid reason to feel this way.

*How do you learn to get around this situation?*

It may take some mental health counseling, attending some mental health support meetings or whatever it is that you can access in your area, but do get some help because it is so important that you can cope.

Without the carer the quality of life of the sufferer would be so much worse.

*It is so important that the carer take care of themselves!  This is an absolute must for the long term health of everybody.  It may mean that you have to take 'time out' somehow, put major restrictions on what is allowable by the sufferer or whatever you choose, but DO TAKE CARE OF YOURSELF.*

## One Of My Worst Times

I learnt the hard way on this one too.

For months my son would not stop drinking heavily and stayed up half the night. He would wake me up at about 1am and then I would be up the rest of the night. In just a few short months my health crashed and I had to make some horrible decisions.

In the end I had to give him an ultimatum to stop drinking so heavily and go to bed earlier or leave. He had nowhere to go so this was a heart wrenching decision on my part, yet from previous discussions I was sure he would move out.

He did move out and he lived on the streets for several months. Sometimes I would see him at night sitting on a park bench in the rain and I would bring him home for a meal and a good sleep, but I still kept the ultimatum in place.

In the end he did find a place to stay but got really unwell because he didn't take his medication and kept drinking heavily.  After a time, a story too long to tell, he ended up in hospital and rehab for just under 2 years.

That's what they call **'tough love'** I guess, but I have never decided who it was tougher for!  It didn't seem to be worrying him too much that he didn't have a roof over his head but it was ripping me apart.

## 12. How does the person with the illness cope?

Well I guess we will never have an answer to this.

### Accepting The Illness

Often the person with the illness will not initially accept that there is an illness and therefore will not co-operate in attending doctors' appointments, taking medication and general well being.

A couple of the reasons that the illness is not accepted by them are because:

- their perception of their world is real as they see it
- they can't understand why we don't understand it

- of facing the stigma that is often attached to mental illness
- they don't want to be seen as not coping
- they don't want to believe they are unwell at all

From what I have been able to ascertain, until there is acceptance by the sufferer then getting the illness under some sort of control is made very difficult indeed.

Because, if they don't take the medication as prescribed you can't tell if it is working or not, whether it needs changing or what needs doing and with them remaining very ill, it becomes very **difficult to make any headway**.

These insidious diseases of the mind can have everyone in turmoil. Not only that, the diseases present in varying degrees of the illness. You may hear of someone having the same illness as your loved one, but their experiences can be quite different.

With schizophrenia a person can go from being calm and relaxed one minute to yelling and screaming the next which can turn the household all upside down.

Paranoia can be quite frightening to live with if someone becomes very ill because you cannot understand what they are thinking.

Disorganized thoughts are very common as well, meaning that it is quite hard to keep up with a conversation at times. They will often walk around talking to themselves which in most cases is conversing with the voices they are hearing. The voices may appear to be from people they know in reality or they may be someone of their own creation.

Bipolar requires another set of coping mechanisms as the sufferer will be manically high then cross over to the depressed state.

I am led to believe that these highs and lows can last for a short period of time or go on for months in either stage and because of these different time lapses bipolar can be difficult to detect, understand and manage.

The mood swings can have a devastating effect on the sufferer, and also the family, as neither party knows how to deal with the situation or which part of the illness they will have to deal with next. The mood swings take a grave toll on the sufferer so get help as soon as possible when you notice something odd is going on. These suffers often have suicidal thoughts.

Depression is an illness that can often be difficult to detect as 'unwell' because people can become so adept at putting on 'a front' of happiness that no-one else knows they are ill. When people suffer very deep depression it can become very debilitating even to the point that they will not leave the house at all.

Suicide can be an out for some people with depression so it is really important to get on to this illness straight away and get help immediately. The stats for suicide are very high and it seems more young men and elderly men are affected than women in the same age groups.

Asperses and Autism effect people in different ways causing management systems to be in place to cope with those illnesses. These illnesses can also have a strain on families but I do not know much about the illnesses themselves. Except to say that from the carers point of view many of the management strategies mentioned need addressing for the long term well being of the family.

## Self Medicating and Addiction

So how do those that are ill cope with these illnesses?

From my understanding from watching and observing people with these illnesses and of carers stories, there is a wide range of coping strategies that are used:

- from hitting the drugs
- alcohol
- self harm and
- suicide

The taking of drugs and alcohol or other substance abuse is referred to as 'self medicating'. In other words they are taking things to get rid of the emotional pain.

If someone has a mental illness and an addiction as well, it is termed 'dual diagnoses'. Time will tell if the supposed addiction is 'self medicating' or if there is an underlying problem there.

My son drank very heavily for about 2 years then cut right back and my thinking now is, that he was going through **a period of coming to terms** with the illness and what it was doing to his life. In other words **'self medicating'** to cope with the pain of being ill. During this time he would swing from agreeing that he had a mental illness to saying there was nothing wrong with him. Whereas now he almost always would agree that he has an illness which has to be dealt with.

When the illness is under some sort of control, keeping busy certainly helps maintain a more positive attitude, but often mixing with other people is not usually to their liking so it is great if they can find interests for themselves.

Part of the coping mechanisms for the ill is to become very, very smart (as in sneaky), and good on them!  But, as carers, we have to become smarter!  Quite a learning curve that one!

If you do have someone ill in your family and they have a dual diagnoses you will need to make a family decision about how you are going to handle the substance abuse (substances are *all* mind altering products).

# 13. Health care

## Personal Hygiene

Some symptoms of the illnesses show as obsessive compulsive disorder (OCD) where the sufferer may be obsessive about the cleanliness of a place or themselves.   This can have just as big an effect on their lives as being unkempt.

Or symptoms may show as total lack of health and personal hygiene which can go from bad to worse. It can be a real struggle to get them to clean themselves or their clothing, because at this time, if they are really ill, they just don't realize they smell so bad and that they look so terrible.  Their bedrooms can be an absolute disaster area, being dirty, smelly, ridden with rotten food and other disgusting odds and ends lying around.

Sometimes we have to try and find a medium where we can cope with it and they will meet us at that level.

## Eating Healthy Meals

I am a believer that a healthy diet is very important and this should be up there on the priority stakes for all the family. It doesn't have to be special but there is strong support in favor of the correct vitamins helping combat some of the effect of mental illness. Vitamin B is often said to be very good for a healthy mind.

Carers too, need to watch their diet so that they will have the strength to keep on keeping on.

Basic good healthy living with plenty of fruit and vegetables, meat, seafood and limited carbohydrates has been suggested as a suitable diet.

For the sufferers:  definite no, no's are coffee, cigarettes, liquor and drugs.

It seems to be a fact though that few people totally give up all these things as much as they would like to, even though they know that it is not good for their health to keep having them.

Because the illness itself causes lack of motivation, and the medication only adds to that problem, their planning for something like food is abysmal.  Also, they have little motivation to cook meals so they grab the first thing they can lay their hands on. Unfortunately, this is not usually something very healthy, usually takeaway, sweet buns, chips or some other fast food which is often very fattening. Or the sugar filled drinks which give them an instant pick-me-up.

I found when my son was very ill he didn't even **know whether he had eaten or not!**

The mental activity can be such a distraction that time means nothing, nor does very much else in their lives at the time.

So, overseeing the health can be something that will benefit everybody. I do remember one doctor saying "don't worry too much about them not eating, sooner or later they will feel hungry enough", and I believe this to be true when they are really ill but on a long term basis this is obviously got to be addressed. When trying to rehabilitate, daily healthy meals are a must.

In the past I have put effort into making a good healthy meal only to have my son say he wasn't hungry and 8 hours later he still hadn't eaten any food.

Pretty typical, huh?

# 14. Family relationships

When dealing with a mental illness in the family it is a very trying time for all concerned.

You have mum who has the nurturing caring thing going on, dad who wants 'to fix it' like the broken window, and the siblings who don't want to know because they are scared they might end up like that too. Alternatively siblings may feel neglected because you, as mum, are spending so much time caring for the person with the illness.

If you have an ill person living with you it is very important to set down guidelines early. I let certain situations go on forever thinking that *it would get better, it would change, it will go away, whatever,* but the true fact is that it was here to stay. I finally realized that if I didn't do something about it things would only get worse, not better. I had to start making decisions and putting guidelines into action.

**Most men find coping with a mental illness very difficult,** mostly because they don't want to believe that they have fathered someone with this condition and secondly because they have the 'fix it' mentality and find that this just doesn't work with a mental illness, so they feel incapable. This feeling then often shows in aggression, frustration and negativity.

Also, they see their wife going through all sorts of stress and can't deal with that either. Another issue here could be that he sees the ill person sitting around all day whilst he goes out to work and this often doesn't go down very well.

As women, we are often, and I hate to say it, too soft in coping with the ill person because we hate seeing our son/daughter/grandchild/spouse/parent suffering so much, even if we don't understand exactly what they are going through. We can still see the agony they have in coping with such an illness.

Family relationships can start falling apart around you and it takes some effort to keep things together.

If this starts to happen then maybe it is time to bring in the mental health counselors to help with a family discussion. It is essential that this is done when problems start arising rather than avoiding problems then trying to solve them once resentment has well and truly set in.

# 15. Self esteem

Most of the medications used for mental illness, or at least schizophrenia and bi-polar, tend to lead to weight gain.

You can guarantee that most sufferers are very aware of the weight they are carrying.

They also understand that they are not behaving the same as most other people.

They really need to feel 'normal' and need their self esteem being pumped up, just like we all do. Praise goes a long way.  But don't expect it back from them because they would probably not be observant enough unless they are fairly well.

My understanding, through observation and discussion with clinicians, is that weight is often put on because of the side effects of the medication, but I have also been led to believe that because the medication makes the sufferer feel so tired they seek junk food and sweet food looking for an energy rush to combat the tiredness. Until a suitable medication dose can be found lethargy can be a real problem, giving the impression of a very lazy person.

As much as I often feel like saying something to the effect of 'you need to lose some weight', I try instead to take the approach of discussing what type of food is being eaten and what type of drinks are being taken.

It works really well if they can get involved in some sort of hobby or such so that they can feel successful at something that they alone have achieved. Usually there are community groups they can attend. Perhaps even a little gardening to get them outside would help.

Without realizing it, things can become a vicious cycle, nagging about health, weight, addictions, tidiness, health care and more. But it is done from a position of caring. The trouble is, the more we nag, the more stressed they become and then the more unwell they become. Then the more we nag. They don't feel as if they are coming up to standard and see this as rejection.

Also if they do care about their family they see themselves as causing a problem around the house and this can be quite distressing for them too.

Social interaction is very hard to maintain after becoming ill, but it is really important that there is encouragement, almost insistence, that this is done early into the rehabilitation because the longer it is before social interaction starts again the harder it will be to activate, even if it just means going out for a coffee or something, not necessarily having to converse with others.

When on the path to a better life there certainly does need to be time out for rest and quiet, but care has to be taken that this time is not just hiding away in front of a TV and not getting involved in other activities. I know we all feel like becoming a 'couch potato' at times, but not all the time.

Although, as mentioned earlier, each situation is different and it will take time to gain the understanding and skills to cope.

# 16. Recovery

First and foremost, there will be no recovery until the person with the illness is ready to take on this task. No matter how hard you try, until they are ready it just will not happen and it is best just to look after their safety and health until such a time evolves. Little nudges along the way certainly won't harm as the more they are exposed to the positive idea of recovery the sooner it may happen.

I will quote from an article written by Helen Glover a woman with a lived experience:

*"Recovery is an active space. Recovery does not simply happen. It cannot rely only on external factors alone such as support, doctors, case managers, hospitalizations, medications or therapies. Recovery requires individual effort, similar in determination, courage and conviction, to*

*the physical effort of an elite athlete. When first diagnosed with a mental illness, I thought that I would find my recovery space by turning up for a doctor's appointment or taking some pills. I did not realize that I had to invest in the process and actually contribute the parts of me that were going to make the journey. Unfortunately and sadly, I doubt that others, especially health professionals, actually expected me to contribute to my recovery process at all."*

But let me assure you that if the person with the illness can come to terms with the fact that they have an illness and are prepared to accept medication then recovery can take a positive turn and most people can start living a meaningful life again.

The time factor might be months for some and years for others, but at least as long as they keep moving towards recovery and can understand why they had a relapse then improvement in their life can make progress. There is a lot to understand about recovery.

In this book I have tried to give a simple outline to caring and guiding a person towards recovery as best I can.

.

## Believe In and Work Towards
## RECOVERY

Over the years my thoughts of a recovery didn't really enter my mind very much.  I was so intent on dealing with the **here and now** that I didn't look too far into the future as I always seemed to be dealing with the present crisis.

I guess if anyone had asked me "will your son ever get well?" I think I probably would have said "no". When I look back it was my lack of knowledge of the illness that would have led me to say "no" because I did not understand that it is an episodic illness. Also, I did not understand that he himself had to come to terms with getting well so that he took the necessary steps in his own life to make it happen.

Medical Science has progressed at such a fast rate over the more recent years and I believe medication will keep improving so that in not so many years to come mental illness will be able to be controlled in a much better way.

At one stage through one of my son's hospitalizations he suffered a couple of 'attacks', similar to epilepsy. It was at this point of time that I started to give up hope that he was ever going to get well.

Funnily enough, this was almost a turning point for him. Whether the whole episode frightened him or what, I am not sure, but from that time onwards he gradually improved in his overall health. Maybe it was like they say, "you have to hit rock bottom before you start making a recovery" and maybe that was his rock bottom.

I know when he was drinking heavily and staying up half the night (about years 3 and 4 after being diagnosed) I used to think rock bottom was going to be jail. Not because he stole but more because he was living a life of not caring for himself or anyone else or their property. Some of his actions were not the best.

Now I am convinced that it is important to believe in 'recovery' and work towards it from the very first day. Live with the belief that it will happen and that it will only be a matter of how and when.

*The numbers of those recovering to some degree are very encouraging and improving all the time.*

**Starting on the Road to Recovery**

It would be really good to start on this road as soon as possible but if someone has suffered a chronic illness then the first thing they need to do is learn to live with the illness and this isn't as easy as it sounds.

*There are so many issues to consider:*

- where are they going to live – it really isn't a good idea for them to live on their own as much as they often will want to because their lifestyle can deteriorate so quickly without proper management
- in saying that it is also not a good idea that they live in an environment where tolerance is not practiced and where negative family issues are taking precedence over the health problems of the person that is ill

- consistency in medication taking, food intake, substance abuse, coffee and cigarettes are all things that, in most cases, can be better controlled under a family situation
- the effects on the family environment
- the effects on the health of the family
- how to handle the stigma that is often associated with a mental illness

**Acceptance that there is an illness in the family**

As much as it is hard for the person with the illness to accept that he/she has an illness, it also is hard for the family to accept and learn to live with this illness within the family circle.

Even more so is the difficulty of finding that you don't really have anyone close to talk to that understands because even your extended family or friends don't understand what you are going through.

Do try and get the extended family involved if they will be, because you will need all the help you can get in the more difficult stages. Just ask, because they probably won't understand otherwise, even if it is just mowing the lawns! Just the fact that some of those household chores are done for you can alleviate your stress levels.

Until the family accepts the situation and then finds out as much as possible about the illness that is being dealt with, any sort of rehabilitation will be very slow and very frustrating.

Recovery from a mental illness will progress at different rates and at different times depending on many things, from medication to relationships and other relevant involvements. It really is a roller coaster ride.

## Mini Relapses and Causes

Once the family is 100% behind a recovery program you will soon see changes for the better. In saying that, as in everybody's life, attitudes and health goes up and down, so do expect that the recovery will be a process of high's and low's.

Often it is from the lows that one discovers what it is that triggers a mini-relapse so it is important to look at this at the time so that early intervention can be made at a future date if this situation occurs again. Treat the lows as a learning curve and talk to the ill person about that and discuss the episode and the lead up to it.

Learning to look for early signs of illness and being able to deal with the episode will make life for everyone go a lot smoother. It took me many years to understand this whole scenario.

Mental illnesses present differently in people due to personalities and other possible causes, so observe and learn as much as you can.

Learn what the side effects of the particular medications are and look for any which are obvious as some of the not so nice side effects can be moderated by other medication that can be prescribed by your doctor. No-one likes the side effects, least of all the person with an illness.

Mini-relapses can be caused by a number of things, often by over stimulation as the person who is ill tries to lead a normal life but brings on the illness again. What I mean by that is that the person with the illness wants more than anything else to be like everybody else, especially if they are in their teens to early twenties. They want to party, drink, go out and generally have a 'wild time' and who can blame them.

The problem with all this is that *the whole getting better routine* goes out the window. If it is just a bit of drinking then it will probably only be a few days before they are back on track again, and in fact, the effects of the drinking may not even present themselves for a couple of day. But if they get into the drugs then it could be a couple of weeks before they are feeling reasonably well again.

Try and be patient and talk it through. It can be really hard to turn around their thinking on this issue though.

A very strong early warning sign of a relapse is if the person who is ill is finding it extremely difficult to get to sleep. This is usually a sign of too much brain activity and it becomes impossible to relax and get to sleep. This needs to be addressed straight away. Deal with it yourselves if you can or contact your psychiatrist/doctor.

## Don't Walk on Eggshells

As I say, as carers we feel hard done by, we lose a lot of our freedom, friends, suffer extra financial costs, deal with stress and tension on an almost daily basis and more.

BUT in the latter years it was not hard to see that my son was suffering much more than I ever did. That was once I got my head out of the sand and understood the illness more.

It is a mother's nature to be overprotective and be a buffer to take away the pain.  This is all well and good, but eventually you realize that if you keep telling a person that they are unwell day in day out, that's exactly what they will be and not only that, they will learn to play on it.  If you can work through this and start encouraging the person to just be one of the family with similar responsibilities.  Try to treat this as a temporary situation and try to keep moving forward towards getting well (I know, a lot easier said than done).

There will be times when compassion is the answer and there will be times when 'tough love' is needed. Tough love is not easy but can be essential in getting things moving in the right direction.

In saying all that, I do believe that nothing will happen until the time arrives when the person who is ill is sick of life as it is and decides to do something about it. Remember the old saying 'you can lead a horse to water, but you can't make it drink'. That is so true, so just hang in there and keep reassuring the person that recovery is possible (though not always so, unfortunately, if someone has been extremely ill for a very long time, or will not practice good health methods) and that you are there to help them on the way.

They will have a much better chance of recovery if they are living in a non-toxic family environment with loving support.

Keep pointing out how far they have come, even if it is only a few small steps.

My son said to me today how good it was to have our present living arrangement - him in the self contained granny flat downstairs. My response with a smile was, "yes, you should listen to your mum more often!" to which he just laughed. Fat chance, I thought!

I had been trying to talk him into this arrangement for about 3-4 years and he would not hear of it. Now that he is ready for it, the arrangement is working really well. Who knows what the future will bring.

**Instigate Routine**

Once the time has come where you think recovery may work start putting everything into place. A little bit of judgment with this will need to be taken.

*Here are some suggestions to better the chances of recovery (it will take time to work through these and make changes, it took me years). Just keep working forward:*

- keep to a strict healthy diet with limited carbohydrates
- reduce sugar intake
- abstain from alcohol and substance abuse
- suggest drinks are decaffeinated coffee, weak tea and fruit juices. Of course, fresh water is the best of all
- check that all medications are taken at the same time each day
- make every effort to get regular hours of sleep, at least 8, but could be as much as 11

- set up a strict exercise routine for every day as this is really important in maintaining general physical and mental well being – someone may need to do this with them
- involve the sufferer in household duties and really push for these duties to be done. Writing a list for each day is recommended so that the chores do not get forgotten.  Start with fairly simple ones, becoming more responsible as the health improves
- try very hard to get some social interaction happening

At first it will seem that there are too many changes to be made and the sufferer may not want to bother. The carer needs to be vigilant to see that these changes are introduced into the daily routine one at a time.  Trying to change everything all at once will be too difficult and before you know it mini relapses will occur.

Initially you will probably find that they will not want to leave the house, not even for things they particularly want to buy. I would suggest you help them through this as it will change.

When my son was quite unwell I used to find that if I asked him to clean up his room or do his dishes they just didn't get done, but when I offered to help he would quite willingly give me a hand. The idea of doing the task on his own seemed insurmountable to him at that stage.

I wish you well on your journey and hope that this book may give you some insight and/or answers to your own situation.

A quote I often remember from another parent I read about says:

*"Those without our troubles only drink the bubbles from the top of a cup of cappuccino whereas I have drunk to the dregs"*

# 17. Acknowledgements

**Helen Glover** is an active trainer, facilitator and consultant in the fields of mental health and recovery, both nationally and internationally. Her work is strongly informed by a lived experience knowledge base of those who have recovered including that of her own recovery from mental illness.

**Health Care Workers and Clinicians on the Sunshine Coast, Queensland, Australia**, who gave their dedicated time to not only helping us on our journey but many others as well and who are responsible for improving the lives of those with a mental illness.

# 18. Disclaimer

This publication is intended to provide helpful and informative material. It is not intended to diagnose, treat, cure, or prevent any health problem or condition, nor is intended to replace the advice of a physician. No action should be taken solely on the contents of this book. Always consult your physician or qualified health-care professional on any matters regarding your health and before adopting any suggestions in this book or drawing inferences from it.

The author and publisher specifically disclaim all responsibility for any liability, loss or risk, personal or otherwise, which is incurred as a consequence, directly or indirectly, from the use or application of any contents of this book.

**Author's Note:**

I need to remind you that I have no medical qualifications and that anything that I have mentioned has been taken from my own life experience in dealing with a son with schizophrenia and as a facilitator for a group of carers of family members with mental illness. I urge all carers to take care of themselves and to seek medical advice if they are at all unable to cope. I also urge them to make every effort to learn as much as they can about the illness they are involved with so that they are better able to cope.

Anything I have mentioned should not be taken as a route to follow but more as something that you could be facing but you should make your own judgment and decisions in relation to your situation.

www.ingramcontent.com/pod-product-compliance
Lightning Source LLC
Chambersburg PA
CBHW071057290526
45795CB00004B/1530